Wisdom on How to Live Life
(Book 3)

Transforming Earth into Heaven

Dr. Tommy S. W. Wong

Dedicated to

my parents, Wong Sze Fong and Woo En Yueh

my parents-in-law, Sum Chip Shing and Ko Luk Ying

my darling wife, Christina

and my wonderful sons, Alston, Lester and Hanson

Acknowledgement

I like to thank the Great Spirit for selecting me as an instrument in authoring this book for the benefit of mankind.

Table of Contents

Chapter 1

Introduction

Humans being the most intelligent species and having lived on Earth for thousands of years, we are yet nowhere near to a life of peace, love, joy and harmony. This book contains a hypothetical story of a young man, Tom, who had a fourth conversation with Guru Harry. This is a continuation of their first three conversations which are contained in the books *"Wisdom on How to Live Life"* and *"Wisdom on How to Live Life (Book 2)"*. Guru Harry epitomizes someone from a spiritual society who offers a way of living which can lead to peace, love, joy and harmony.

In this fourth conversation, Guru Harry expounded his spiritual wisdom on:

(1)   why it is easier to communicate in spirit,

(2)   why we should take responsibility for our actions,

(3)   why we should live our lives according to our wishes,

(22) why masters do not do bad deeds,
(23) why people are not receptive to the "new" consciousness,
(24) how to build a loving society, and
(25) how to bring heaven to Earth,

Through this fourth conversation, young Tom is even more prepared and wiser on how to live his life.

Wisdom on how to live life

Chapter 2

Fourth Conversation with Guru Harry (Part 1)

Hello Guru Harry, I'm back.

Hello Tom, welcome back.

I'm so glad that I can communicate with you in spirit.

Yes, I'm glad that I can communicate with you too.

No, I mean I thought it would be so sad not to be able to see you in your body.

I don't have a body now. You mean you are not sad.

No, I'm not because I find that it's so much easier to communicate with you in spirit.

How much easier?

I mean I can communicate with you anywhere, anytime I like. I don't have to locate your body physically.

Yes, spiritual communication is wonderful.

Yes, it really is. I mean it's so much better than physical communication.

And it's more truthful.

Absolutely. We can just say it out straight without worrying about this and that.

Sure, you don't have to worry about anything. Just say what you feel.

Right. I feel like saying it's wonderful to be here communicating with you.

Me too.

What's more I can feel the communication.

Feeling is the language of the soul.

Soul language.

This is why there's no need to grieve when our loved ones pass on.

You mean we can always communicate with them spiritually.

I mean they are always around spiritually.

Forever and a day.

Amen.

How wonderful it'll be if our loved ones are always around.

They are always around.

Then life is wonderful.

Life is always meant to be one-derful.

But life on Earth is not wonderful now?

You are right.

Why is it so?

Like I said in our first conversation, what life is like on Earth really depends on what people do there.

What do people do?

They are not making life easy for themselves.

They are not?

In fact, life on Earth is getting harder and harder.

Yes, you are right. It is getting harder and harder every year.

Yep, and it'll get harder and harder every month.

Guru Harry, why is life so difficult?

It doesn't have to be difficult.

But life is difficult now, why?

Because our world operates on the basis of competition and with a "wrong" focus.

Like economic growth?

Like economic growth.

How can life be easier?

Realize our true form.

Which is?

We're souls and not bodies.

Yes, we've heard this thousands of years ago and you've also said it in our previous conversations.

Yes, I did.

But life is still so hard, and in fact, it's getting harder and harder.

It's because many have heard the saying but few practice it.

Practice what?

If we realize that we're souls, then we will practice "we are all one".

There's only one of us.

Then there's no need to compete.

There's no sense to compete.

We will then cooperate.

Cooperation is better than competition.

And we will have win-win solutions rather than lose-lose situations.

Yes, with competitions, there are no winners.

Only losers.

And there's no sense to make life difficult for others.

Why not?

Because if life is difficult for others, it's also difficult for ourselves.

Because there's only one of us.

That's why it's very important to practice "we are all one".

Guru Harry, this is all very nice philosophically, but how can we really make life easier physically?

Provide basic physical needs.

Which are?

Air, water, food, clothing and shelter.

How about healthcare?

Well if the society can afford it, they can also provide healthcare.

But you mean it's not necessary.

You see if we follow the divine laws, there shouldn't be any illness.

We certainly don't follow the divine laws.

You've made a very important observation.

I did?

You see if we don't follow the divine laws, how can we expect to be well?

We're not well.

Exactly. Our society expects us to be sick.

Our society expects all of us to be sick.

We're all sick.

It's a sick society.

And we have clinics and hospitals everywhere.

And our society is proud to have clinics and hospitals everywhere.

They think it's a sign of success.

Actually it's a sign of failure.

Only sick societies are proud to have clinics and hospitals everywhere.

How about a spiritual society?

Do you recall the focus of a spiritual society?

Physical and spiritual well being of their citizens.

Well remembered.

So, everybody is well.

So, there is no need for clinics and hospitals.

So, there is no need for healthcare.

And then there're masters in spiritual society.

Yes.

They live to a ripe old age.

So, they are old.

And they can choose to leave their bodies when their bodies are still healthy.

Amazing!

I mean our bodies are designed by the Divine, right?

Right.

So, how can there be any illness?

So if we live in line with the divine laws, there won't be any illness.

A world free of illness.

Sounds like heaven on Earth.

Yes, Earth can be heaven. So, do you think all the basic needs can be provided?

Since we produce so many non-basic items, surely we can produce less non-basic items so that we produce enough basic items for everybody.

Then everybody's basic needs are satisfied.

Then we don't have to worry about our basic needs.

You know Tom, this is in fact the secret in building a loving society.

All love and no fear.

Yes, when all the basic needs are satisfied, there'll be no fear.

Then we'll have a loving society.

Then we'll evolve spiritually.

Then it'll be heaven on Earth.

There's another point about satisfying the basic needs.

What is it?

You see for most people, they are prepared to work during their entire working life.

Yes, this is actually the definition of working life.

Then, they hope that their earnings will be more than sufficient to cover the basic needs.

This sounds reasonable.

So that they can save for their retirement.

This sounds reasonable too.

Is this too much to ask?

Asking for what?

To be able to work throughout the working life and have enough savings for retirement.

This sounds very reasonable.

But what happens if this cannot be achieved?

You mean the savings are not enough for retirement.

Money is not enough.

Then the poor soul has to worry.

Then the old soul cannot retire in peace.

Then the poor soul cannot die in peace.

Then the old soul cannot rest in peace.

Then the society also cannot be in peace.

Precisely! This in fact should be the criterion in assessing whether a society is "successful" or not.

What is the criterion?

The standard of living of the bottom stratum of society.

But they usually talk about the standard of living of the top stratum or at best, of the middle stratum of society.

Yes, they don't talk about the bottom stratum.

Why is it?

Shame.

Yes, the standard of living of the bottom stratum is usually shameful.

But this is the stratum where the standard of living should be raised.

Why?

Because people are usually worried about what is the lowest level that they can fall to.

So if the lowest level is raised to a reasonable level?

Then fear is removed from the society.

Then we'll have a fearless society.

Then we'll have a caring society.

Then we'll have a loving society.

Then we'll have heaven on Earth.

So how can we raise the standard of living of the bottom stratum of society?

Well how much wealth does the top stratum have?

Plenty.

How much is plenty?

More than enough to live ten life times?

More than that. More than enough to live one hundred life times.

Really?

Do you know how distorted the wealth distribution is on Earth?

How distorted?

For the first time in human history, one person can own more wealth than an entire nation.

Wow, this is really distorted.

So, the gap between the rich and the poor is getting wider.

The gap between the rich and the poor is very wide.

The gap between the rich and the poor is too wide.

It's too wide for comfort.

The poor are very uncomfortable.

And the top stratum is very comfortable.

So they can help the bottom stratum to live a more comfortable life.

When they help others, they help themselves.

Because we are all one.

Then why don't we build a loving society?

Body consciousness.

Can you elaborate?

You see if we perceive we're bodies only, we'll be only concerned with the survival of the body.

We'll be only concerned with the survival of our own body.

So we won't care about others.

Who cares?

So we'll be only concerned with making ourselves richer.

And the others poorer.

The rich get richer and the poor get poorer.

This is exactly what is happening in our society.

I know.

How do you know?

I was there.

Isn't it sad?

Actually, it's cruel.

So humans are not divine.

They are more like demons.

So humans are worse than animals.

And there's an interesting irony.

What is it?

Humans put all their efforts in trying to keep the body going.

And?

And yet the body can go anytime.

It can be here today and gone tomorrow.
Exactly. So all their efforts are fruitless.

So they put all their efforts into nothing.

So actually it's better to be kind to others.

It's better to care about others.

Then humans can be divine.

But humans are not divine now.

That's why life is getting harder and harder.

Are there any other reasons why life is getting harder?

Technology.

I thought that technology makes life easier.

Appropriate use of technology makes life easier.

So we're not using technology appropriately?

Let me put it this way.

Which way?

With the new technology, are people buzier at work or do they have more time for leisure?

Undoubtedly, buzier at work.

But technology is supposed to give us more time for leisure?

It is?

So technology makes us buzier and our lives harder.

So life is hard.

And there's another point.

What is it?

Since the world operates on the basis of competition, it's like a race.

We are all racing.

And the fastest runners dictate the rate of technology advancement.

So the rate is very fast?

The rate is too fast.

Too fast for the other runners.

So the other runners are struggling to catch up.

They'll never catch up. So life becomes a struggle.

And it's getting harder and harder.

This is a very good observation, Guru Harry. So how can we make life easier?

Slow down and cooperate.

You mean we should all walk at a pace that we're comfortable with.

Yes, and then we're all winners.

This is what you said in our first conversation.

Well remembered.

So, it'll be all winners and no losers.

A world full of winners.

Sounds like heaven on Earth.

Yes, Earth can be heaven.

Are there other reasons why life is getting harder?

Resources.

Resources? What do you mean?

Actually, I mean cheap resources.

Can you elaborate?

You see, in the earlier generations, human population was small and resources were aplenty.

So resources were cheap.

But with successive generations, resources are getting depleted.

So less and less resources.

So resources are getting more expensive.

So life is getting harder.

And the human population is exploding.

So we need more resources.

And the resources are diminishing.

So we are getting a double whammy.

So the resources are getting doubly more expensive.

And life is getting doubly hard.

And with the current trend, life will get harder and harder.

Guru Harry, is there a way to make life easier?

By consuming less and using renewable resources.

But our societies like to consume more.

Actually, they should consume less, and be mindful of future generations.

But our societies are consuming like there's no tomorrow.

With the way our societies are consuming, there won't be a tomorrow.

So how can we have a tomorrow?

By consuming less and using renewable resources.

Are there other reasons why life is getting harder?

There're too many things.

You mean there're too many desires.

Life is getting too complicated.

Life is getting too hard.

Yes, life will be hard when it gets complicated.

So how can we make life easier?

Live a simple life.

That's what masters do, right?

That's what masters do. In fact, they live a very simple life.

How simple?

There're masters who only live on bread and water.

Really?

And then there're masters who live alone in a cave for more than a decade.

How extraordinary!

It's better to live with less.

I was told that the more the better.

Actually, it's the less the better.

Also, why doesn't our society broadcast about these masters?

Because our society is more interested in material enrichment than spiritual enlightenment.

So the masters live with minimal material wealth?

So they live with practically nothing.

And yet they live like having millions.

When you can live with nothing, you are richer than millionaires.

You are richer than billionaires.

And you can live in spiritual bliss.

And we can all live in divine bliss.

Hallelujah!

And it'll be heaven on Earth.

And there's one more point about living with nothing.

What is it?

You see, the masters are not afraid of living with nothing.

So they are not afraid of dying with nothing.

You see, when you can live with nothing, you have no fear.

So the masters have no fear.

So they live a fearless life.

What a wonderful way to live!

Indeed. This is the way to live.

This is the way to god.

We'll all become god.

We're all god.

Amen.

But do we really die with nothing?

Actually, it's impossible to die with nothing.

That's why the masters are not afraid of dying with nothing?

That's why they are not afraid of living with nothing.

What do we have when we die?

We've our souls.

And the Great Spirit.

Now let me share with you a saying.

What is it?

Money comes and goes; morality comes and grows.

So we should grow our morality rather than money.

Yet our society grows money rather than morality.

So our society is rich in money but poor in morality.

Actually, it would have been better if our society is rich in morality and poor in money.

How much better?

You see there's a problem with money.

What is it?

You could lose it overnight.

How can that be?

Disaster can hit anybody anytime.

It happens all the time.

And it can be a man-made or natural disaster.

And all the money is gone.

But nobody can take away your morality.

We can keep it for life.

You can even keep it in the afterlife.

So it's better to have morality than money.

So it's better to be poor and moral than rich and immoral.

So our society is moving in the "wrong" direction?

Well, do we have peace on Earth?

No, there's no peace on Earth.

Do we have heaven on Earth?

No, there's no heaven on Earth.

Yes, our society is moving in the "wrong" direction.

Actually, why do we live such a complicated life?

Because many are caught up with the pleasures of the senses.

Can you elaborate?

You see to enjoy the pleasures of the senses, you need many things.

So pleasures of the senses lead to a complicated life.

So pleasures of the senses lead to a painful life.

So life is painful without joy.

Life is meant to be joyful.

So how can we have a joyful life?

Enjoy the pleasures of the soul.

Can you elaborate?

You see, to enjoy the pleasures of the soul, you need nothing.

So we can live with nothing?

Well apart from the basic needs of the body, we can live with nothing.

Because the soul needs nothing.

That's why spiritual societies provide the basic physical needs and then let their citizens evolve spiritually.

That's why they live on Earth as though it's heaven.

Yes, Earth can be heaven.

So live a simple life.

And life will be wonderful.

But life is not wonderful now.

You are right, and do you notice an interesting irony?

What is it?

Humans are supposed to be the most intelligent species on Earth.

Yes.

And they have lived on Earth for thousands of years.

Yes.

Yet many are still living without the basic needs.

Yes, it's an irony except it's not interesting but tragic.

Yes, it's tragic to see people dying from hunger everyday.

Yes, it's tragic to see people dying from hunger every hour.

And nobody seems to care.

Nobody cares.

Humans are supposed to be divine beings and yet their behavior is more like demons.

So we're moving closer to hell instead of heaven.

So we have hell on Earth instead of heaven on Earth.

So how can we have heaven on Earth?

Practice "we are all one".

Chapter 3

Fourth Conversation with Guru Harry (Part 2)

Guru Harry, can I ask you what life is like with a body and then without a body?

Yes, you can.

What is life like with a body and then without a body?

When you are with the body, it's like being in school.

You mean the school of life.

I mean you'll learn and then face problems.

So life is hard.

Actually learning is fun.

So life is fun.

Life is meant to be fun.

But life is not fun now?

You are right.

Why is it?

Because they have taken the fun out of learning.

So there is no fun.

But this is only happening in "normal" schools.

What do you mean?

You see in "normal" schools, students only learn for the sake of passing examinations.

So there is no fun.

So it's fun-less.

Yes, we have discussed education in our first conversation.

And it's not achieving what education is supposed to achieve.

What is education supposed to achieve?

To educate students to become humane beings and enlightened souls.

How about in the school of life?

In the school of life, learning is fun because we learn skills that are actually useful for going through life.

So life is fun.

And this is how you grow.

How do I grow?

You grow by learning how to solve problems.

What happens if I can't solve the problems?

Just like in a school, the teacher will present problems to you that are appropriate to your abilities.

So if I can't solve the problem, the teacher will help.

So if you face problems in life, the Great Spirit will help.

So I'll solve the problems.

Actually you know, the problems are already solved.

Really?

When the teacher presents the problems to you, he already has the solutions.

Wow, so the problems can definitely be solved.

But there's one catch.

What is the catch?

The solutions may not be to your expectations or to your liking.

So we may not see solutions as solutions or we may not implement the solutions.

Exactly!

So actually there're no problems.

Only solutions.

But there're many problems on Earth and the solutions don't seem to be there?

The solutions are there, except they are not implemented.

Name one solution.

Practice "we are all one".

You are right. We're definitely not implementing this solution.

No, you are not.

What will happen if we did?

There'll be peace on Earth.

There'll be heaven on Earth.

Earth will become heaven.

So why don't we implement it?

Body consciousness.

Yes, you've explained this earlier. So when we live with the body, we learn to solve problems.

This is the period of growth.

Then, what is life like without a body?

When you are without the body, it's like a school break.

You mean it's like a school holiday.

Yes, you can relax and take life easy.

We can all relax and take life easy.

But there's one disadvantage.

What is it?

There won't be growth.

Why is it?

Because there aren't any problems to solve.

So we only grow if there are problems.

And we don't grow when there aren't problems.

So we should welcome problems?

Bingo, you've hit the jackpot!

Really? What is the jackpot?

We shouldn't see problems as problems. We should see them as opportunities for growth.

That's what masters do, right?

That's what masters do.

So the more problems we encounter, the more we grow.

So the more problems we encounter, the faster we grow.

So is it better to live with a body?

But you've to solve problems.

So is it better to live without a body?

But there won't be growth.

Sounds like we're in a lose-lose situation.

Actually, we're in a win-win situation.

How is it?

You see with the cycle of life, we'll live with a body and grow a little, and then we'll live without a body and rest a little.

Then?

Then we'll live with another body and grow a little, and then we'll live without a body and rest a little.

Then?

Then we'll repeat the cycle again.

Then?

Then we'll repeat the cycle again.

Until when?

Eternity.

You mean we don't grow out of it?

Nope.

Then how do we go to heaven?

Maybe there's no heaven.

Oh yes, that's what you said in our last conversation.

Right. There's nowhere else to go.

So we're stuck in this cycle of life.

So we can enjoy this cycle of life forever.

Isn't it boring?

Isn't it wonderful?

What is so wonderful?

We can grow.

So what happens when we grow so much that we actually reach enlightenment?

Well enlightenment isn't a destination, you know.

What do you mean?

You see when something grows, it'll continue to grow.

So it'll grow and grow.

So we'll grow and grow.

Even after we reach enlightenment?

Even after we reach enlightenment.

You mean there is no end.

Why should there be an end?

I thought there should be an end so that we can stop growing.

Do you know what happens when you stop growing?

What?

End of life.

Which is?

Death.

What death?

I don't mean physical death.

What do you mean?

I mean death of the soul.

But the soul never dies.

Exactly. That's why we'll continue to grow.

Anyway, I thought when we become enlightened, we go to heaven and then we don't come back.

Let me put it this way.

Which way?

You see with the concept of life, we may believe that we only live on Earth temporarily. When we reach enlightenment, we'll leave Earth and then go to another place.

Like heaven?

Like heaven.

Yes, this is the traditional theological teaching.

Or we may believe that life is a cycle in which we'll return to Earth continuously.

This is new to me.

Well, which concept of life will make Earth a better place to live in?

I would say the second because I've to come back again and again.

That's why it's better to believe that we'll be in this cycle forever.

That's why it's better to believe that we're all in this cycle together.

That's also why Earth is in such a mess.

Why?

Because too many are thinking that they can make a mess on Earth and then they can leave and go to another place.

Like heaven?

Like heaven.

How can they go to heaven if they make a mess on Earth?

By believing.

By believing in what?

Believing that they can make a mess on Earth and yet still go to heaven.

How can anyone teach such a belief?

Those who like large groups of followers.

You mean people like this kind of teaching.

I mean people like to go to heaven.

But this kind of teaching is detrimental to the followers.

And to planet Earth.

You mean nobody cares?

Who cares?

But really, how can anybody believe that after making a mess on Earth, they still deserve to go to heaven?

There're two points here.

What is the first point?

Many will claim that they didn't make the mess even if they did.

And the second?

Many will take things even though they don't deserve them.

Wow Guru Harry, you are really describing people in our society.

I know.

How do you know?

I was there.

So, many like this belief?

Well, it's an easy way out, isn't it?

Is it?

I mean if we say you've to be good and perfect before you can go to heaven, then how many can go?

Few and far between.

Very few and far between.

Right but it's only because they don't deserve to go.

Exactly. That's why they reject this concept and believe the easier one.

Which is?

They can still go to heaven after making a mess on Earth.

But the masters don't teach this kind of teaching, right?

Nope, they don't teach this kind of teaching.

Thank God for that.

Because true masters don't look for large groups of followers.

What do they look for?

They look to develop others to become masters.

So there'll be more masters.

True masters are not those who have large followings. They are the ones who have developed more masters.

So more masters and less followers.

And everybody can become a master.

Wow, what happens when everybody is a master?

There'll be peace on Earth.

There'll be heaven on Earth.

And there's a saying.

What is it?

I'm God and you are God.

So we're all God?

Right. True masters look at everybody as their equals.

So we're all masters?

At least we can all become masters.

So what do masters teach?

Live a disciplined and humane life.

Can you elaborate?

A disciplined life means putting your senses under control.

And a humane life?

A humane life means only doing good and no harm to others.

Sounds like it's a hard life.

You know there's a saying.

What is it?

If you look for an easy life, your life will be hard. If you are prepared for a hard life, your life will be easy.

So life is easy for the masters because they are prepared for a hard life.

Life can be easy for all of us if we're prepared for a hard life.

At last, life can be easy!

And Earth can be heaven.

Guru Harry, I'm so glad that you told me there's no heaven.

Yes, it's better to believe that there's no heaven.

Then, we won't be running away from Earth.

Then, we won't be running to heaven.

Then we'll put in more effort to transform Earth.

Then we'll put in more effort to transform ourselves.

Then Earth will be heaven.

Do you see the importance of beliefs?

Yes, I do. Different beliefs give diametrically opposite outcomes.

That's why we should choose our beliefs carefully and wisely.

But how?

When you choose your belief, ask one question.

What is the question?

Does it bring love or fear?

If it brings love?

Then, the belief is spiritually sound.

You mean it's in line with the divine laws?

Yes, it's in line with the Divine.

Amen.

There's another point related to believing there's heaven.

What is the point?

You see, if we believe there's heaven.

Okay.

How would we feel when we left our bodies and found out that there's no heaven?

Disappointed.

How disappointed?

Extremely, because we've waited an entire life time to get there.

You know this is exactly what happened to many souls.

What happened?

They were told that there was heaven and then subsequently found out that there wasn't one.

Who told them?

Religion.

How did they find out?

After they left their bodies, they found that there is no heaven to go to.

They must have been very disappointed.

Extremely, they were also disappointed with the religious teaching.

How disappointed were they?

They vowed that if they had known that there wasn't a heaven, they would have lived their lives differently.

How differently?

They would do good just for the sake of doing good and not look for a reward like going to heaven.

Right. The reward for doing good is in the doing.

Right. When we do good, we're in heaven on Earth.

So we don't look for heaven in our afterlife.

There's no heaven in our afterlife.

No heaven and no hell.

This is all there is.

This is all there'll be.

Forever and a day.

Amen.

Are there other things you'd like to ask me?

Oh sure, I still have many things to ask you.

Ask and you shall be answered.

You know to every problem, there can be physical solutions.

And there can be spiritual solutions.

Yes, which one is better?

Let me put it this way.

Which way?

Suppose you are interested in buying a car.

Okay.

How can you find the money to pay for the car?

I can work and make some money to pay for the car.

Do you like your work?

Well I may not like it but I've to do it so that I can get money.

Many people live their lives this way, right?

Which way?

They endure their unhappiness during work so that they can gain happiness after work.

Is this wrong?

It's not a question of right or wrong, but there's a better way.

Which is?

Be happy at work so that you don't have to look for happiness after work.

Sounds too ideal. It doesn't happen in our society.

It doesn't happen in a materialistic society.

Why?

Because they value money higher than happiness, and they have a "wrong" concept about work.

What is the "wrong" concept?

They see work as a means to make money.

Everybody sees work as a means to make money.

Not in a spiritual society.

How do they see work?

An opportunity to serve others.

Wow, so it's not about making money.

It's not even about ourselves.

It's to do with others.

So it's about "Your gain is my gain".

So everybody gains.

A world full of gainers.

What a wonderful way to live!

Life is meant to be one-derful.

Because we are all one.

Shall we get back to buying the car?

Yes, I'd like to buy a car.

Suppose you don't want to wait for your money from work, how else can you find the money?

I can borrow.

From where?

Credit card.

Yes, many borrow money from their credit card, so that they can buy what they like and get their happiness instantly.

Is this okay?

You are actually trading instant happiness for deferred suffering.

Suffering?

By borrowing, you have to work longer to pay for the same car because of the interest on the credit card.

Is this wrong?

This is childish psychology.

Childish psychology?

You see if you ask a child to choose between a sweet and a ten dollar note.

He will choose the sweet.

Right, because the sweet gives him instant happiness.

You mean we shouldn't choose the sweet.

I mean we should grow out of our childish thinking and choose wisely.

So that we can become old and wise.

You know there are many old and un-wise.

Really? Why is it?

There're many misguided souls on our planet.

So how can be become old and wise?

Or just wise.

Oh yes, we don't have to be old to be wise.

Spiritual education.

Like what was said in this and the previous conversations?

Yes, like what was said in this and the previous conversations.

Can we get back to buying the car?

Sure. Suppose now you don't want to borrow money and also you don't want to work, how else can you get the money?

Steal?

You know this may be the best option.

Really?

You see if you steal and you don't get caught, then you don't have to work for the money.

So this is the best option?

But there's one catch.

What is the catch?

You've to live with the consequences according to the divine laws.

So this is not the best option.

So these are the physical solutions to buying the car.

Right. Is there a spiritual solution?

Yes, there is and it's a tricky one.

What is it?

Be happy without the car.

What? So we won't have the car?

Live happily without the car.

So we don't buy the car.

So there's no need to find the money.

So there's no need to work unhappily.

And souls don't have needs.

So we live with less desire.

Less desire, more peace.

Peace is better than happiness as a goal in life.

Yes, we've discussed this in our first conversation.

Yes, we did.

And there's a major advantage in the spiritual solution.

What is it?

You see with the physical solutions, they don't last.

They don't?

After you've got one car, some time later you'll want a bigger car.

After we've got a bigger car, some time later we'll want even a bigger car.

So one car after another and so it goes on.

There's no end to desire.

Unless there is.

So what happens when there is no end to desire?

Unhappiness.

How about the spiritual solution?

While the physical solutions cannot last, the spiritual solution is long lasting.

How long?

It can last forever.

That's really long.

And there's one more disadvantage with the physical solutions.

What is it?

What happens if the car you bought is an expensive car?

I'll be very proud of my car.

What happens if your car gets a dent?

I'll be very upset.

Can you prevent your car from getting a dent?

I'll do my best.

How sure can you be that your car won't get a dent?

I cannot be sure.

So are you worried?

Yes, I'm worried.

You see, physical solutions bring worry and fear.

Is this why people in materialistic society have so much fear?

All fear and no love.

So how can we remove fear?

Live spiritually.

Live a life of no desire.

Then, you'll live in peace.

Then, there'll be peace on Earth.

Then, Earth will be heaven.

Wisdom on how to live life

Chapter 4

Fourth Conversation with Guru Harry (Part 3)

Guru Harry, can we now discuss spiritual solutions to problems in life?

Sure, no problem.

Yes, I wish there're no problems but actually, there're many problems in life.

Remember, see problems as opportunities for growth and not as problems?

Yes, I remember but this is easier said than done.

Okay, you know you can actually encounter problems and don't see them as problems.

How?

Problems that you've solved before.

Well yes, if I encounter problems that I've solved before, I won't see them as problems because I already know the solutions.

Exactly. That's why you should solve more problems.

So when we solve more problems, there'll be fewer problems.

And when you solve all the problems, there'll be no problems.

No problems. You mean like heaven on Earth.

And there's one more point about problems.

You mean there're problems?

How can you encounter a big problem and don't see it as a big problem?

How?

By having encountered a bigger problem.

So after we've encountered a huge problem, all the other problems appear small.

Exactly. That's why you should welcome problems, the bigger the better.

That's what the masters do, right?

That's what the masters do.

But I'm really having problem with my problems.

Okay, let's see what problems you have.

Okay, let me start with the one for which I already know the answer.

Yes, it' good to start with the one for which you already know the answer.

Death.

Okay, what is the spiritual solution to death?

The solution is to believe that we're souls and not bodies.

And then?

Then, souls do not die. They live forever. So we actually cannot die.

How does this belief help the living?

By believing that we cannot die, we don't fear death. And by not fearing death, we don't fear life.

Yes, splendid answer. And by not fearing life, you can really be alive in your life.

But many are not really alive.

Good observation.

Why is it?

Because they live in fear.

Fear of what?

Fear of life and fear of afterlife.

Can you elaborate?

You see, our society teaches us to keep our bodies going for as long as possible, this is actually teaching us to fear death.

So?

So if we fear death, then we fear life.

How about the afterlife?

Religion teaches us to fear the afterlife.

How do they do that?

Hell and eternal damnation.

Wow, this is really fearful.

Yes, in fact it's hard to imagine a greater fear.

So religion is instilling the greatest fear in humans?

This is why there's so much fear on Earth.

Because we got hit by a double whammy.

Fear from secular society and fear from religious society.

But I thought religion is supposed to teach love.

Unfortunately, they teach fear, like fear of God.

I thought we should love God.

Yes, we should love God and fear sin.

So they are not doing what they are supposed to do.

It's worse than that.

In what way is it worse?

You see many think that religious teaching is about love.

Of course.

So what happens when they teach fear?

We'll think fear is love.

And love is fear.

So we're completely confused.

This is why there's so much confusion on Earth.

So it's all fear and confusion on Earth?

This is also why there's so much violence on Earth.

Because fear creates violence.

In fact, we're probably still within the most violent period of human history.

So how can we bring peace to Earth?

Practice love.

But what is love?

Excellent question.

Really?

Yes, with all the "wrong" teachings, it's hard to know what love really is.

No, we don't know.

Then, practice "we are all one".

Oh yes, this concept is easier to understand and more practical.

So, whatever you do, think of the other person first.

Do unto others as you would have them do unto you.

Whatever is good for others, is good for ourselves.

So, do good, see good, and be good.

For "we are all one".

This is the way to god.

This is the way to love.

Love all, serve all.

Let's go to the next problem.

Illness.

Okay, what about illness?

We're fearful of illness.

Why?

There're three parts to this fear.

What is the first part?

We're fearful that it can't be cured.

Then?

Then we'll die.

So?

So we're fearful of death.

So we're back to the fear of dying.

Of course, because this has been the teaching for thousands of years.

Well, you have to grow out of it.

How?

Spiritual education.

Like what was said in this and the previous conversations?

Yes, like what was said in this and the previous conversations.

And the second part of fear is physical discomfort.

So it's to do with the body.

Yes, it's to do with the body.

So it's body consciousness.

Yes, we're concerned with the body.

More than the soul.

Yes, because we're living with the body everyday.

Until you lose it.

This is why we don't want to lose it.

Until you do.

What do you mean?

When you lose your body, you'll find that it's not a big deal.

But that will be too late, right?

Exactly. So live with the body but don't put too much emphasis on it.

You mean put more emphasis on the soul.

Right, much more emphasis on the soul.

So we won't be too concerned with physical discomfort.

So we can be completely unconcerned with physical discomfort.

That's what the masters do, right?

That's what the masters do.

And the third part of fear is the high cost of medical treatment which can become a financial problem.

Again, see problems as growth opportunities rather than problems.

What do you mean?

Do you take good care of your body?

I do the best I can.

Do you exercise financial prudence?

I do the best I can.

Then whatever financial problem you encounter, it's probably for your spiritual growth.

So there's no need to worry?

You know there's a saying.

What is it?

Do the best you can, and leave the rest to God.

Yes, I'm leaving everything to God.

And there's another point.

What is it?

Whatever financial problem you may encounter, do you think God can solve it?

God is all powerful; of course he can solve it.

So what is the problem?

But I don't know whether she'll solve it for me.

But you and God are one.

So my problem is his problem.

There's only one of us.

We are all one.

So have faith in God.

Deep faith.

Now, let me share with you something on medical cost.

Okay, what is the cost?

You know there are hospitals that do all kinds of operations.

Yes.

But do you know that there are hospitals that do operations for free?

You mean they do them completely free of charge.

Yes, not a penny.

Amazing!

And they exist on Earth right now.

Wow, you mean we've heaven on Earth?

So the medical cost can be zero.

Wow, we really have heaven on Earth.

Now, let me share with you something on the curing of illness.

Okay, what is the cure?

Do you know that there're masters who can cure illness just by a single touch?

Amazing.

They can also do remote healing and even raise the dead.

Out of this world!

And these masters are living on Earth right now.

So they have come to bring heaven to Earth?

Indirectly.

How?

They have come to help humans to bring heaven to Earth.

Why don't they just bring heaven to Earth directly?

You know what will happen if they did bring heaven to Earth directly?

Earth will soon go back to hell like what we've now.

Exactly. That's why they have come to transform humans.

Humans certainly need a transformation.

A major transformation.

All the way from demonic.

To human.

And then to divine.

Do you have other problems?

Job.

Yes, what about job?

More specifically, being jobless.

Yes, in your society, there are problems with jobs and there are problems with being jobless.

Can you elaborate?

In your society, you are using jobs as a means to make money so that you can satisfy the basic physical needs.

So?

So even if you are unhappy at your job, you'll still do it.

Yes, I'll do it.

So, you become unhappy.

Yes, I'm unhappy.

And if many are unhappy?

We'll have an unhappy society.

Now if you become jobless, the situation gets worse.

Yes, it gets worse.

Now even your basic needs cannot be satisfied, so you'll be even more unhappy.

Very unhappy.

So, irrespective of whether you've a job, or you are jobless, you are unhappy.

A world full of unhappiness.

This is happening on Earth right now.

Guru Harry, you are right. So how can we have a happy world?

Let everybody's basic needs be satisfied first.

And then?

And then use the job as a means to serve others.

I'm happy serving others.

And then even if you are jobless, your basic needs are satisfied.

So, I'm happy.

So, irrespective of whether you've a job, or you are jobless, you are happy.

A world full of happiness.

Are there other things you'd like to ask me?

Sure, Guru Harry, you know in our third conversation, you said that we've to take responsibility for all our actions.

Why? Shouldn't we?

I mean life will be so much easier if we don't have to take on responsibility.

Okay, let me put it this way.

Which way?

You see the world is in a mess right now.

Yes, a huge mess.

Who caused the mess?

I'm not sure.

But somebody caused it, right?

Right.

Did anybody own up?

Nobody.

So why don't they own up?

Because they don't want to take the responsibility.

Right. If people don't take responsibility for their actions, they'll take irresponsible actions.

Wow, is this why the world is in such a big mess right now?

You bet.

But taking responsibility sometimes can mean pain.

But it's good for your soul.

And by avoiding responsibility, we can also avoid pain.

But you can't avoid the consequences of your actions.

Why not?

Divine laws.

Who cares about the divine laws?

You are right.

I am?

Look at the world right now.

I see what you mean.

This is the consequence of not taking responsibility.

A hugh consequence. So Guru Harry, how can we get out of this mess?

Take responsibility for our actions

But many don't want to take responsibility.

They'll learn.

They will?

They'll come back to this mess again and again.

Until they learn.

Until they clear up the mess.

But what if they don't come back?

They have to come back.

Why?

Because there's nowhere else to go.

You mean there is no heaven.

This is all there is.

Oh yes, that's what you said in our third conversation.

So, they have to come back.

They have to come back again and again.

Actually after they clear up the mess, it'll be heaven.

Wow that'll be good. We come back to heaven again and again.

We can come back to heaven from heaven.

Heaven here, heaven there, heaven everywhere.

There's another point about taking action?

What is it?

Your actions should be your expressions of your wishes to the world.

So I should do according to my wishes.

Right, but many do not do according to their wishes.

What do you mean?

Their actions are according to somebody else's wishes.

Such as?

Student studies medicine because teacher wishes him to.

Daughter marries Jack because mother wishes her to.

Son works in China because father wishes him to.

Everybody keeps quiet because government wishes them to.

So for many, they don't live their lives according to their wishes.

They live their lives according to somebody else's wishes.

So they'll live in regret.

And they can't live in peace.

And they'll try to live their lives through their children's lives.

And their children can't live in peace.

Unless their children live their lives according to their wishes.

But why don't people live their lives according to their wishes?

Because they don't want to take responsibility and are afraid of results.

What do you mean?

Because they can't be sure how things will turn out.

All of us can't be sure how things will turn out.

Exactly. That's why there're so few people living their lives according to their wishes.

So how can we have more people living their lives according to their wishes?

Commit to the action, and not the result.

Can you elaborate?

Take the action as an end in itself. Don't take it as a means to a result.

So we don't use the action as a means to a reward.

Take the action as the reward and accept whatever result it produces.

That's what masters do, right?

That's what masters do.

So live our lives according to our wishes and take responsibility for our actions.

And there's one more thing?

What is it?

Never consider yourself a victim.

What do you mean?

Never think that what happens to you is due to somebody else's action.

Some incidents are caused by others right?

They may appear so on the physical plane. But on the spiritual plane, it is to our advantage to believe that everything happens to us is our own choosing.

So we can never be victims.

Unless we choose to.

In which case, we're not really victims.

The greatest advantage of this belief is that it gives us empowerment.

Empowerment to change the situation.

Exactly. So live a life of empowerment, young man.

Yes, sir.

And transform Earth into heaven.

Yes, sir.

And Earth shall be heaven.

Chapter 5

Fourth Conversation with Guru Harry (Part 4)

Guru Harry, can I ask you something which has puzzled me for a long time?

Let's see if I can solve your puzzle.

I see some people who do a lot of good deeds and then they do one bad deed.

Intriguing.

Yes, it is. Why is this so and is the person good or bad?

Let me put it this way.

Which way?

Suppose a person has done one hundred good deeds and one bad deed, is he good or bad?

Yes, this is what I want to know.

What is the common perception?

The common perception is that the person is good.

Why?

Because of one hundred minus one, the person has done ninety-nine good deeds.

You are right with the common perception but the common perception is "wrong".

Really? Can you explain?

You see, let us suppose the person does one good deed a day.

This is good.

So for one hundred days, he has been doing good.

This is very good.

But on the one hundred and first day, he did a bad deed.

This is bad.

So having done good deeds for one hundred days, why did he do a bad deed on the one hundred and first day?

This is the puzzle.

You see all deeds start with a thought.

Yes, thought, word and deed.

So for the person who did the bad deed, he had to have a bad thought.

This is bad.

The question is then since he has been doing good for one hundred days, where did the bad thought come from?

Yes, where did it come from?

And since he has been doing good everyday, wouldn't it be more natural for him to do good on the one hundred and first day?

Yes, it would be more natural.

But he did a bad deed.

Indeed he did.

Isn't it strange?

Very strange.

Well, maybe he had the bad thought all along.

He is bad.

He may be using his good deeds to cover his bad deed.

This is bad indeed.

So his motivation for doing good may not be good.

No good.

You see if you look at the masters.

Yes, I'm looking.

They do good all the time.

Yes, they do.

Do they do one hundred good deeds and one bad deed?

They do one thousand good deeds and zero bad deeds.

Why don't they do bad deeds?

Because they don't have bad thoughts.

Why don't they have bad thoughts?

Because they are good.

Right. Good people don't have bad thoughts and therefore don't do bad deeds.

Masters don't have bad thoughts and therefore don't do bad deeds.

It's impossible for them to have bad thoughts.

It's impossible for them to do bad deeds.

What will happen if everybody does good deeds only?

There'll be only good on Earth.

So, all good and no bad.

It'll be heaven on Earth.

Now there's another common misconception.

What is it?

If Mr. A did one hundred good deeds and one bad deed, and Mr. B did only ten good deeds, who is better?

By simple mathematics, Mr. A is better because he did a net of ninety-nine good deeds while Mr. B did only ten good deeds.

This is the common misconception. You see you are correct in your mathematics, but incorrect in your assessment.

Can you explain?

You see what will happen if everybody behaves like Mr. B?

There'll be only good on Earth.

So, all good and no bad.

It'll be heaven on Earth.

What will happen if everybody behaves like Mr. A?

There'll be good and bad on Earth.

In fact, there's another serious consequence?

What is it?

We won't know when Mr. A will do good and when he will do bad?

But with Mr. B, we'll know that he'll always do good.

So who is better?

I'll say Mr. B, and there'll be heaven on Earth.

Yes, young Tom, you see it's very unnatural for a good person to do bad.

But it's natural for a bad person to do good.

So that he'll look good.

But actually he is no good.

Do you remember the god-man I talked about in our second conversation?

You mean Mr. A is a dishonest god-man?

These are the most dangerous people on Earth.

What happens when these people are around?

There'll be no peace on Earth.

We don't have peace on Earth now.

Because our society perceives Mr. As as good and there're too many of them around.

So how can we have peace on Earth?

Realize that Mr. As are bad and Mr. Bs are good.

So we'll only do good.

So, we'll be good, see good, and do good.

This is the way to god.

There's another point about doing good.

What is it?

Do you think our society likes Mr. B?

Of course our society likes Mr. B.

You'll be surprised. Actually our society doesn't like Mr. B.

Unthinkable.

If you look at masters who have walked on this Earth.

Yes, I'm looking.

How many were condemned?

Many.

What did our society do to them?

They killed them.

Are Mr. Bs the masters?

Yes, they are.

So does our society like Mr. B?

I'm shocked and horrified.

Yes, humans can be horrible.

Humans can be demonic.

Or they can be divine.

How could they kill the masters?

They do it all the time.

But why do they kill the masters?

You see in our second conversation, I mentioned that like attracts like.

Yes and you mentioned that dishonesty attracts dishonesty.

So dishonesty doesn't like honesty.

You mean dishonesty cannot tolerate honesty.

It's like heaven and hell.

They cannot co-exist.

And there's another point.

What is the point?

Are masters divine?

Of course they are.

So they killed the Divine.

In the name of God.

You see how confused humans are.

No wonder Earth is in a mess.

In a big mess.

So how can we get out of this mess?

Realize that we're divine.

So that we don't kill the Divine.

Then, there'll be peace on Earth.

Then, there'll be heaven on Earth.

In all these killings, do you notice a divine phenomenon?

What is the phenomenon?

The masters willingly gave up their bodies.

Because they know they are not their bodies.

We're not our bodies.

Yes, we're souls and not bodies.

103

And the masters manifest their divinity by giving up their bodies.

Yes, the masters are divine.

We're also divine.

So we can also willingly give up our bodies for a good cause.

And this leads to one other point if you decide to do good.

What is the point?

Prepare to be condemned.

Wow, what a revelation. We've always been told if we do good, everybody likes us.

Well, our society has not reached that stage yet.

When will our society reach that stage?

When everybody does good.

So when we do good, we'll be condemned.

We've got to do good despite condemnation.

Why?

To transform Earth into heaven.

That's what the masters do, right?

That's what the masters do.

Guru Harry, I've another puzzle.

Let's see if I can solve your puzzle.

What you've said makes so much sense to me. Why are some people not receptive to your ideas?

Yes, it's puzzling.

That's right. This is the puzzle. Why aren't they receptive to your ideas?

Old consciousness.

Old what? Can you explain?

Okay. Let's suppose we come into this world like an empty cup.

So we're empty.

As we go through life, our cup is being filled.

So we're getting filled.

After many years, our cup is full.

So we're full.

What happens when the cup is full, and we continue to fill it with water?

The water will overflow.

Will the 'new' water go into the cup?

How can the 'new' water go into the cup? It is already full of 'old' water!

Is it any use to continue to pour 'new' water into the cup?

No, it's useless.

So how can we fill the cup with 'new' water?

We need to throw away the 'old' water.

Exactly. So how can people be receptive to the 'new' consciousness?

They need to throw away the 'old' consciousness.

Will this be a problem?

It'll be a problem to some because they have been taught the 'old' consciousness for thousands of years.

Has the 'old' consciousness brought peace to Earth?

No peace on Earth. There's only violence.

So, is the 'old' consciousness working?

Certainly not!

Well, then it's time to empty our cup and fill it with something new.

Like the 'new' consciousness?

Like the 'new' consciousness.

Wow Guru Harry, thank you for all the spiritual wisdom. I'm much better prepared to live my life and to transform Earth into heaven.

Yes, young Tom, live a fearless life.

Yes, sir.

Live a loving life.

Yes, sir.

And live a blissful life.

Yes sir, for the Great Spirit and I are one.

Goodbye, Tom!

Goodbye, Guru Harry!

Index

About the author

Dr. Tommy S. W. Wong (back cover of this book) is a civil engineer by training, and is a renowned hydrologist worldwide. He is also a personal growth consultant, and has authored engineering, spiritual and self-help books. Dr. Wong lives spiritually in the midst of modern Singapore. He is committed to bringing engineering and spiritual teachings to the world for the benefit of mankind. Further information about Dr. Wong's work can be found on his http://wisdomlife.page4.me/.

Selected books by Tommy S. W. Wong

Wong T.S.W. (2009) "How Sai Baba Attracts Without Direct Contact," CreateSpace, Scotts Valley, CA, USA, 108 pp.

Wong T.S.W. (2010) "Wisdom on How to Live Life," CreateSpace, Scotts Valley, CA, USA, 154 pp.

Wong T.S.W. (2010) "Wisdom on How to Live Life (Book 2)," CreateSpace, Scotts Valley, CA, USA, 110 pp.

Wong T.S.W. (2010) "Wisdom on How to Live Life (Book 3)," CreateSpace, Scotts Valley, CA, USA, 124 pp.

Wong T.S.W. (2011) "How Sai Baba Attracts Without Direct Contact (Book 2)," CreateSpace, Scotts Valley, CA, USA, 102 pp.

Wong T.S.W. (2011) "Wisdom on How to Live Life (Book 4)," CreateSpace, Scotts Valley, CA, USA, 122 pp.